Creepy Creatures

Ants

Sue Barraclough

Heinemann LIBRARY

Little Nippers

www.heinemann.co.uk/library
Visit our website to find out more information about **Heinemann Library** books.

To order:
☎ Phone 44 (0) 1865 888066
▤ Send a fax to 44 (0) 1865 314091
▭ Visit the Heinemann Bookshop at www.heinemann.co.uk/library to browse our
catalogue and order online.

First published in Great Britain by Heinemann
Library, Halley Court, Jordan Hill, Oxford OX2
8EJ, part of Harcourt Education.
Heinemann is a registered trademark of Harcourt
Education Ltd.

Editorial: Sarah Shannon and Louise Galpine
Design: Jo Hinton-Malivoire and bigtop,
Bicester UK
Picture Research: Hannah Taylor and
Sally Claxton
Production: Camilla Smith

Originated by Dot Gradations
Printed and bound in China by South China
Printing Company

ISBN 0 431 93260 3 (hardback)
09 08 07 06 05
10 9 8 7 6 5 4 3 2 1

ISBN 0 431 93265 4 (paperback)
09 08 07 06 05
10 9 8 7 6 5 4 3 2 1

British Library Cataloguing in Publication Data
Barraclough, Sue
595.7'96
Creepy Creatures: Ants
A full catalogue record for this book is available
from the British Library.

Acknowledgements
The publishers would like to thank the following
for permission to reproduce photographs: Alamy
Images pp. 23 (Chris Fredriksson), 10 (Holt
Studios International Ltd), 12 (Roger Eritja); Ardea
pp.4, 6, 7 top, 14-15, 17 (Steve Hopkin), 16
(Pascal Goethegluck); Corbis pp.22 (Antony
Bannister/Gallo Images), 21 (George D.Lepp);
Ecoscene p.13, 8-9 (Paul Franklin); FLPA p.11
(Minden); Garden Matters pp.18-19 (John
Feltwell); Imagestate p. 9 top; NHPA pp. 7 bottom
(Ant Photo Library), 5 (Stephen Dalton); Science
Photo Library pp. 20-21 (Sinclair Stammers).

Cover photograph of an ant, reproduced with
permission of Corbis/ Ralph A. Clevenger.

Every effort has been made to contact copyright
holders of any material reproduced in this book.
Any omissions will be rectified in subsequent
printings if notice is given to the publishers.

The paper used to print this book comes from
sustainable resources.

Contents

Ants

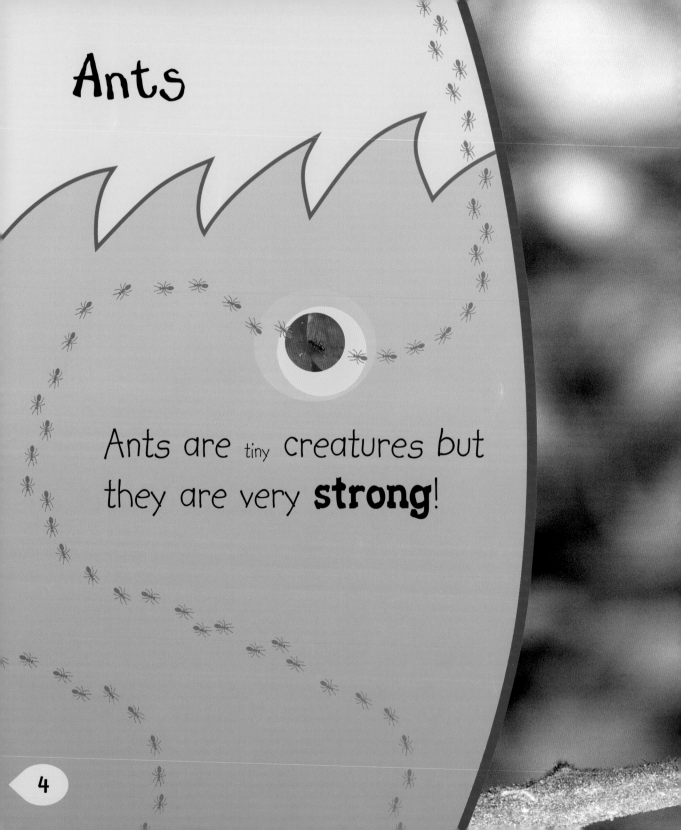

Ants are tiny creatures but they are very **strong**!

Different ants

There are many different types of ants.

Looking for ants

Ants can be found in woods and gardens...

...and even in your home – especially near food!

An ant's body

Ants are insects. They have three parts to their bodies.

thorax

head

abdomen

They have six legs. Can you count them all?

Ants have two antennae for touching and feeling.

antennae

They use them to find out if other ants are friends or enemies.

Mighty ants

Ants have **strong**, sharp jaws for biting and cutting.

They can carry things that weigh much more than they do.

Ants' homes

Ants live in big groups called colonies.

They build nests in warm, safe places

15

Queen ant

Every colony of ants has a queen.
The queen lays the eggs.

The eggs grow and change into larvae.

larvae

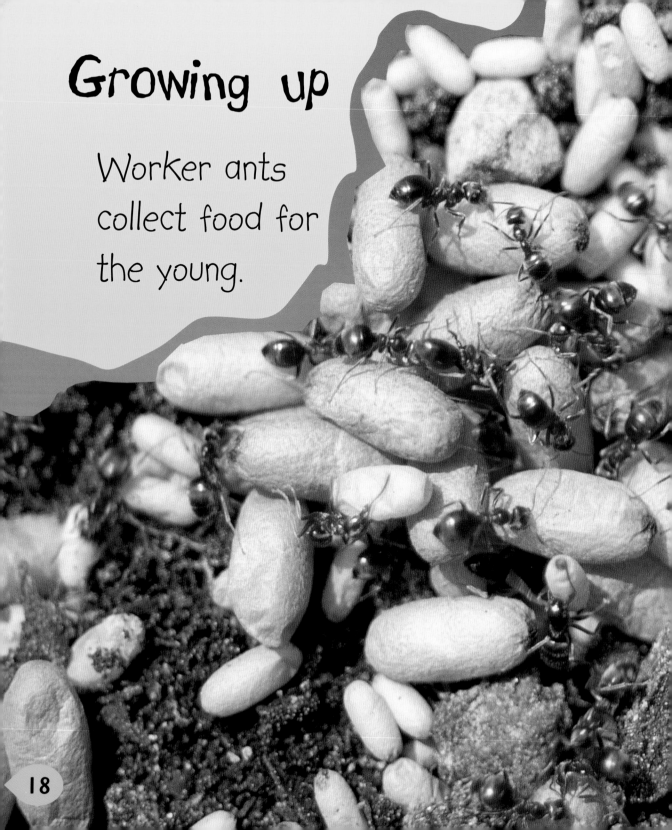

Growing up

Worker ants
collect food for
the young.

They look after
the young as they

grOW
and
change.

Food for ants

Ants follow trails left by other ants to help them find **food**.

farmer ant

aphid

Some ants farm aphids. Ants like to eat the sweet honeydew aphids make.

21

Ants in danger

If the nest is in danger, the ants will carefully move the eggs to safety.

Many different kinds of animal like to eat ants.

23

Index

Notes for adults

This series supports the young child's exploration of their learning environment and their knowledge and understanding of their world. The four books when used together will enable comparison of similarities and differences to be made. (N.B. Many of the photographs in **Creepy Creatures** show the creatures much larger than life size. The first spread of each title shows the creature at approximately its real life size.)

The following Early Learning Goals are relevant to the series:
• Find out about, and identify, some features of living things, objects, and events that they observe
• Ask questions about why things happen and how things work
• Observe, find out about, and identify features in the place they live and the natural world
• Find out about their local environment and talk about those features they like and dislike.

The books will help the child extend their vocabulary, as they will hear new words. Since words are used in context in the book this should enable the young child gradually to incorporate them into their own vocabulary. Some of the words that may be new to them in **Ants** are *thorax, abdomen, antennae, colonies, larvae,* and *aphids.*

The following additional information may be of interest:
Ants can lift objects that are fifty times their own weight, which is thought to be the equivalent of a person lifting a small car. It is possible to observe a colony of ants by turning over large stones or rotten logs. The light and air will alert the ants to danger and they will immediately go into action to move the queen and the eggs to safety further undergound. Aphids, such as greenfly and blackfly, produce a sugary waste (honeydew) as they feed on plants. Ants 'farm' groups of aphids by protecting them from danger and predators and even moving them to new plants to feed on. This means that they can collect the honeydew to feed themselves and their young.

Follow-up activities
Children might like to follow up what they have learned about ants by making their own observations in parks and gardens. Develop ideas and understanding by discussing any features they find interesting, and encourage children to record their observations and ideas in drawings, paintings, or writing.